Great Works

Instructional Guides for Literature

Of Mice and Men

A guide for the novel by John Steinbeck
Great Works Author: Kristin Kemp

SHELL EDUCATION

Publishing Credits

Corinne Burton, M.A.Ed., *President*; Emily R. Smith, M.A.Ed., *Content Director*; Lee Aucoin, *Multimedia Designer*; Stephanie Bernard, *Assistant Editor*; Don Tran, *Production Artist*; Amber Goff, *Editorial Assistant*

Image Credits

Shutterstock (cover)

Standards

© 2007 Teachers of English to Speakers of Other Languages, Inc. (TESOL)
© 2007 Board of Regents of the University of Wisconsin System. World-Class Instructional Design and Assessment (WIDA)
© Copyright 2010. National Governors Association Center for Best Practices and Council of Chief State School Officers. All rights reserved.

Shell Education

5301 Oceanus Drive
Huntington Beach, CA 92649-1030
http://www.shelleducation.com
ISBN 978-1-4807-8508-3
© 2015 Shell Educational Publishing, Inc.

Table of Contents

How to Use This Literature Guide 4
    Theme Thoughts. 4
    Vocabulary. 5
    Analyzing the Literature 6
    Reader Response. 6
    Close Reading the Literature. 6
    Making Connections 7
    Creating with the Story Elements. 7
    Culminating Activity 8
    Comprehension Assessment. 8
    Response to Literature 8

Correlation to the Standards. 8
    Purpose and Intent of Standards 8
    How to Find Standards Correlations. 8
    Standards Correlation Chart. 9
    TESOL and WIDA Standards 10

About the Author—John Steinbeck 11
    Possible Texts for Text Comparisons 11

Book Summary—*Of Mice and Men*. 12
    Cross-Curricular Connection 12
    Possible Texts for Text Sets 12

Teacher Plans and Student Pages. 13
    Pre-Reading Theme Thoughts 13
    Section 1: Chapter 1 14
    Section 2: Chapter 2 24
    Section 3: Chapter 3 34
    Section 4: Chapter 4 44
    Section 5: Chapters 5–6 54

Post-Reading Activities 64
    Post-Reading Theme Thoughts 64
    Culminating Activity: Lights, Camera, Action! 65
    Comprehension Assessment. 67
    Response to Literature: Equality for All 69

Answer Key 71

How to Use This Literature Guide

Today's standards demand rigor and relevance in the reading of complex texts. The units in this series guide teachers in a rich and deep exploration of worthwhile works of literature for classroom study. The most rigorous instruction can also be interesting and engaging!

Many current strategies for effective literacy instruction have been incorporated into these instructional guides for literature. Throughout the units, text-dependent questions are used to determine comprehension of the book as well as student interpretation of the vocabulary words. The books chosen for the series are complex exemplars of carefully crafted works of literature. Close reading is used throughout the units to guide students toward revisiting the text and using textual evidence to respond to prompts orally and in writing. Students must analyze the story elements in multiple assignments for each section of the book. All of these strategies work together to rigorously guide students through their study of literature.

The next few pages will make clear how to use this guide for a purposeful and meaningful literature study. Each section of this guide is set up in the same way to make it easier for you to implement the instruction in your classroom.

Theme Thoughts

The great works of literature used throughout this series have important themes that have been relevant to people for many years. Many of the themes will be discussed during the various sections of this instructional guide. However, it would also benefit students to have independent time to think about the key themes of the novel.

Before students begin reading, have them complete *Pre-Reading Theme Thoughts* (page 13). This graphic organizer will allow students to think about the themes outside the context of the story. They'll have the opportunity to evaluate statements based on important themes and defend their opinions. Be sure to have students keep their papers for comparison to the *Post-Reading Theme Thoughts* (page 64). This graphic organizer is similar to the pre-reading activity. However, this time, students will be answering the questions from the point of view of one of the characters in the novel. They have to think about how the character would feel about each statement and defend their thoughts. To conclude the activity, have students compare what they thought about the themes before they read the novel to what the characters discovered during the story.

How to Use This Literature Guide *(cont.)*

Vocabulary

Each teacher overview page has definitions and sentences about how key vocabulary words are used in the section. These words should be introduced and discussed with students. There are two student vocabulary activity pages in each section. On the first page, students are asked to define the ten words chosen by the author of this unit. On the second page in most sections, each student will select at least eight words that he or she finds interesting or difficult. For each section, choose one of these pages for your students to complete. With either assignment, you may want to have students get into pairs to discuss the meanings of the words. Allow students to use reference guides to define the words. Monitor students to make sure the definitions they have found are accurate and relate to how the words are used in the text.

On some of the vocabulary student pages, students are asked to answer text-related questions about the vocabulary words. The following question stems will help you create your own vocabulary questions if you'd like to extend the discussion.

- How does this word describe _____'s character?

- In what ways does this word relate to the problem in this story?

- How does this word help you understand the setting?

- In what ways is this word related to the story's solution?

- Describe how this word supports the novel's theme of . . . .

- What visual images does this word bring to your mind?

- For what reasons might the author have chosen to use this particular word?

At times, more work with the words will help students understand their meanings. The following quick vocabulary activities are a good way to further study the words.

- Have students practice their vocabulary and writing skills by creating sentences and/or paragraphs in which multiple vocabulary words are used correctly and with evidence of understanding.

- Students can play vocabulary concentration. Students make a set of cards with the words and a separate set of cards with the definitions. Then, students lay the cards out on the table and play concentration. The goal of the game is to match vocabulary words with their definitions.

- Students can create word journal entries about the words. Students choose words they think are important and then describe why they think each word is important within the novel.

How to Use This Literature Guide (cont.)

Analyzing the Literature

After students have read each section, hold small-group or whole-class discussions. Questions are written at two levels of complexity to allow you to decide which questions best meet the needs of your students. The Level 1 questions are typically less abstract than the Level 2 questions. Level 1 is indicated by a square, while Level 2 is indicated by a triangle. These questions focus on the various story elements, such as character, setting, and plot. Student pages are provided if you want to assign these questions for individual student work before your group discussion. Be sure to add further questions as your students discuss what they've read. For each question, a few key points are provided for your reference as you discuss the novel with students.

Reader Response

In today's classrooms, there are often great readers who are below-average writers. So much time and energy is spent in classrooms getting students to read on grade level that little time is left to focus on writing skills. To help teachers include more writing in their daily literacy instruction, each section of this guide has a literature-based reader response prompt. Each of the three genres of writing is used in the reader responses within this guide: narrative, informative/explanatory, and argument. Students have a choice between two prompts for each reader response. One response requires students to make connections between the reading and their own lives. The other prompt requires students to determine text-to-text connections or connections within the text.

Close Reading the Literature

Within each section, students are asked to closely reread a short section of text. Since some versions of the novels have different page numbers, the selections are described by chapter and location, along with quotations to guide the readers. After each close reading, there are text-dependent questions to be answered by students.

Encourage students to read each question one at a time and then go back to the text and discover the answer. Work with students to ensure that they use the text to determine their answers rather than making unsupported inferences. Once students have answered the questions, discuss what they discovered. Suggested answers are provided in the answer key.

How to Use This Literature Guide *(cont.)*

Close Reading the Literature *(cont.)*

The generic, open-ended stems below can be used to write your own text-dependent questions if you would like to give students more practice.

- Give evidence from the text to support . . . .
- Justify your thinking using text evidence about . . . .
- Find evidence to support your conclusions about . . . .
- What text evidence helps the reader understand . . . ?
- Use the book to tell why _____ happens.
- Based on events in the story, ...
- Use text evidence to describe why . . . .

Making Connections

The activities in this section help students make cross-curricular connections to writing, mathematics, science, social studies, or the fine arts. Each of these types of activities requires higher-order thinking skills from students.

Creating with the Story Elements

It is important to spend time discussing the common story elements in literature. Understanding the characters, setting, and plot can increase students' comprehension and appreciation of the story. If teachers discuss these elements daily, students will more likely internalize the concepts and look for the elements in their independent reading. Another important reason for focusing on the story elements is that students will be better writers if they think about how the stories they read are constructed.

Students are given three options for working with the story elements. They are asked to create something related to the characters, setting, or plot of the novel. Students are given a choice in this activity so that they can decide to complete the activity that most appeals to them. Different multiple intelligences are used so that the activities are diverse and interesting to all students.

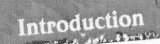

How to Use This Literature Guide (cont.)

Culminating Activity

This open-ended, cross-curricular activity requires higher-order thinking and allows for a creative product. Students will enjoy getting the chance to share what they have discovered through reading the novel. Be sure to allow them enough time to complete the activity at school or home.

Comprehension Assessment

The questions in this section are modeled after current standardized tests to help students analyze what they've read and prepare for tests they may see in their classrooms. The questions are dependent on the text and require critical-thinking skills to answer.

Response to Literature

The final post-reading activity is an essay based on the text that also requires further research by students. This is a great way to extend this book into other curricular areas. A suggested rubric is provided for teacher reference.

Correlation to the Standards

Shell Education is committed to producing educational materials that are research and standards based. As part of this effort, we have correlated all of our products to the academic standards of all 50 states, the District of Columbia, the Department of Defense Dependents Schools, and all Canadian provinces.

Purpose and Intent of Standards

Standards are designed to focus instruction and guide adoption of curricula. Standards are statements that describe the criteria necessary for students to meet specific academic goals. They define the knowledge, skills, and content students should acquire at each level. Standards are also used to develop standardized tests to evaluate students' academic progress. Teachers are required to demonstrate how their lessons meet standards. Standards are used in the development of all of our products, so educators can be assured they meet high academic standards.

How to Find Standards Correlations

To print a customized correlation report of this product for your state, visit our website at http://www.shelleducation.com and follow the online directions.
If you require assistance in printing correlation reports, please contact our Customer Service Department at 1-877-777-3450.

Correlation to the Standards (cont.)

Standards Correlation Chart

The lessons in this book were written to support today's college and career readiness standards. The following chart indicates which lessons address each standard.

College and Career Readiness Standard	Section
Read closely to determine what the text says explicitly and to make logical inferences from it; cite specific textual evidence when writing or speaking to support conclusions drawn from the text. (R.1)	Close Reading the Literature Sections 1–5; Analyzing the Literature Sections 1–5; Making Connections Section 1
Determine central ideas or themes of a text and analyze their development; summarize the key supporting details and ideas. (R.2)	Analyzing the Literature Sections 1–5; Reader Response Sections 1–5; Post-Reading Response to Literature
Analyze how and why individuals, events, or ideas develop and interact over the course of a text. (R.3)	Analyzing the Literature Sections 1–5; Creating with the Story Elements Sections 1–5
Interpret words and phrases as they are used in a text, including determining technical, connotative, and figurative meanings, and analyze how specific word choices shape meaning or tone. (R.4)	Vocabulary Sections 1–5
Read and comprehend complex literary and informational texts independently and proficiently. (R.10)	Entire Unit
Write arguments to support claims in an analysis of substantive topics or texts using valid reasoning and relevant and sufficient evidence. (W.1)	Reader Response Sections 1, 3–4; Analyzing the Literature Sections 1–5; Close Reading the Literature Sections 1–5; Post-Reading Response to Literature
Write informative/explanatory texts to examine and convey complex ideas and information clearly and accurately through the effective selection, organization, and analysis of content. (W.2)	Reader Response Sections 1–2, 4–5; Making Connections Section 5; Post-Reading Response to Literature
Write narratives to develop real or imagined experiences or events using effective technique, well-chosen details and well-structured event sequences. (W.3)	Reader Response Sections 2–3, 5; Creating with the Story Elements Sections 1, 3–5; Post-Reading Response to Literature
Produce clear and coherent writing in which the development, organization, and style are appropriate to task, purpose, and audience (W.4)	Reader Response Sections 1–5; Making Connections Section 5; Post-Reading Response to Literature
Develop and strengthen writing as needed by planning, revising, editing, rewriting, or trying a new approach. (W.5)	Post-Reading Response to Literature
Conduct short as well as more sustained research projects based on focused questions, demonstrating understanding of the subject under investigation. (W.7)	Analyzing the Literature Sections 1–5; Reader Response Sections 1–5; Making Connections Section 2; Post-Reading Response to Literature

Correlation to the Standards (cont.)

Standards Correlation Chart (cont.)

College and Career Readiness Standard	Section
Draw evidence from literary or informational texts to support analysis, reflection, and research. (W.9)	Post-Reading Response to Literature
Write routinely over extended time frames (time for research, reflection, and revision) and shorter time frames (a single sitting or a day or two) for a range of tasks, purposes, and audiences. (W.10)	Reader Response Sections 1–5; Post-Reading Response to Literature
Prepare for and participate effectively in a range of conversations and collaborations with diverse partners, building on others' ideas and expressing their own clearly and persuasively. (SL.1)	Culminating Activity
Adapt speech to a variety of contexts and communicative tasks, demonstrating command of formal English when indicated or appropriate. (SL.6)	Culminating Activity
Demonstrate command of the conventions of standard English grammar and usage when writing or speaking. (L.1)	Entire Unit
Demonstrate command of the conventions of standard English capitalization, punctuation, and spelling when writing. (L.2)	Entire Unit
Apply knowledge of language to understand how language functions in different contexts, to make effective choices for meaning or style, and to comprehend more fully when reading or listening. (L.3)	Reader Response Sections 1–5; Post-Reading Response to Literature
Determine or clarify the meaning of unknown and multiple-meaning words and phrases by using context clues, analyzing meaningful word parts, and consulting general and specialized reference materials, as appropriate. (L.4)	Vocabulary Sections 1–5
Acquire and use accurately a range of general academic and domain-specific words and phrases sufficient for reading, writing, speaking, and listening at the college and career readiness level; demonstrate independence in gathering vocabulary knowledge when encountering an unknown term important to comprehension or expression. (L.6)	Vocabulary Sections 1–5

TESOL and WIDA Standards

The lessons in this book promote English language development for English language learners. The following TESOL and WIDA English Language Development Standards are addressed through the activities in this book:

- **Standard 1:** English language learners communicate for social and instructional purposes within the school setting.

- **Standard 2:** English language learners communicate information, ideas and concepts necessary for academic success in the content area of language arts.

About the Author—John Steinbeck

Using his native home of California as inspiration for many of his works, John Steinbeck contributed over 25 novels, nonfiction books, and short story collections to American literature, several of which are considered classics.

Born on February 27, 1902, Steinbeck enjoyed a comfortable childhood with his parents and three sisters. He had a horse named Jill who was the inspiration for his short story, *The Red Pony*. He developed a passion for writing in his early teens and even contributed to his school's newsletter.

Steinbeck attended Stanford University off and on for five years, but he did not graduate. Determined to earn a living as an author, he published his first book, *Cup of Gold*, in 1929. It was disappointing to both critics and readers. Undeterred, he continued writing and published his first successful novel, *Tortilla Flat*, in 1935. The novels *In Dubious Battle*, *Of Mice and Men*, and *The Grapes of Wrath* followed within the next five years. These books, sometimes called the "California Novels," all take place in California during the Great Depression and focus on the plight of migrant workers. Other success followed Steinbeck as the stage production of *Of Mice and Men* opened in 1937, and the novel *East of Eden* was turned into an Academy Award-winning film in 1955.

Steinbeck was awarded many prestigious honors during his writing career. In 1940, he received the Pulitzer Prize for his novel, *The Grapes of Wrath*. In 1962, he was given a Nobel Prize for Literature, and in 1964 was awarded the Presidential Medal of Freedom by Lyndon B. Johnson.

Steinbeck was married three times. He was married to Carol Henning from 1930–1943. He and his second wife, Gwyndolyn Conger, were married from 1943–1948 and had two sons named Thomas Steinbeck and John Steinbeck IV. His third and final wife was Elaine Anderson Scott to whom he was married from 1950 until his death.

By the mid-1960s, his health had declined after suffering mini-strokes and congenital heart failure. He died on December 20, 1968. His novels continue to leave legacies even decades after his death. *Of Mice and Men* and *The Grapes of Wrath* remain two of the most-often taught novels for high school students.

Possible Texts for Text Comparisons

The other books in Steinbeck's "California Novels" would be enriching texts for readers as they are all set in California and involve migrant workers. These titles include: *Tortilla Flat*, *In Dubious Battle*, and *The Grapes of Wrath*.

Book Summary—*Of Mice and Men*

George and Lennie are an unlikely pair making their way from job to job as migrant workers in California during the 1930s. George is small and intelligent, while Lennie is a gentle giant with intellectual disabilities. In a life where men travel alone and watch out only for themselves, they are a family. Their dream is to own a small farm where they can grow food, raise rabbits, and, as Lennie says, "live off the fatta the lan.'"

Their dream seems within reach when they stumble upon their next employment opportunity. There they meet the other workers, including Candy, an old man with money saved in the bank. He offers to contribute his savings to George and Lennie's dream in exchange for the food and shelter the small farm will provide.

The trio needs to bide their time for a month so that they can earn the remaining money needed to buy the land. However, trouble is lurking around the farm in the form of the boss's son, Curley, and his wife. Curley is a small, angry man who starts fights and bullies Lennie; his wife is an unhappy and provocative flirt who fascinates Lennie.

One night, George ventures out with some of the other workers and leaves Lennie at the farm. Lennie gets involved in a violent encounter with Curley's wife that leads to a tragic end to this story of friendship.

Cross-Curricular Connection

This book could be used in a social studies unit on the Great Depression, the Dust Bowl and its aftermath, or migrant workers. It could also be used to help students learn about and empathize with people who have intellectual disabilities.

Possible Texts for Text Sets

- Gregory, James N. *American Exodus: The Dust Bowl Migration and Okie Culture in California*. Oxford University Press, 1991.
- Hesse, Karen. *Out of the Dust*. Great Source, 2009.
- Lansdale, Joe R. *All the Earth, Thrown to the Sky*. Delacorte Books for Young Readers, 2011.
- Mavridis, George. *Joanna, God's Special Child*. Outskirts Press, 2013.

Name _____

Date _____

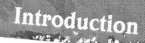

Pre-Reading Theme Thoughts

Directions: Read each of the statements in the first column. Decide if you agree or disagree with the statements. Record your opinion by marking an X in Agree or Disagree for each statement. Explain your choices in the fourth column. There are no right or wrong answers.

Statement	Agree	Disagree	Explain Your Answer
You can make your dreams come true by working hard.			
It is better to be with others than to be by yourself.			
Sometimes there is no good solution to a problem.			
People with intellectual disabilities should not be responsible for their actions.			

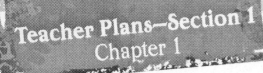
Vocabulary Overview

Ten key words from this section are provided below with definitions and sentences about how the words are used in the book. Choose one of the vocabulary activity sheets (pages 15 or 16) for students to complete as they read this section. Monitor students as they work to ensure the definitions they have found are accurate and relate to the text. Finally, discuss these important vocabulary words with students. If you think these words or other words in the section warrant more time devoted to them, there are suggestions in the introduction for other vocabulary activities (page 5).

Word	Definition	Sentence about Text
foothill (ch. 1)	a low hill at the bottom of a mountain	The golden **foothill** curves up to the mountain.
junctures (ch. 1)	the places where things join	The trees carry debris in their lower leaf **junctures**.
recumbent (ch. 1)	lying down	The sycamore trees' **recumbent** branches arch over the water.
tramps (ch. 1)	people who travel on foot begging or looking for jobs	The path is beaten down by **tramps** looking for water.
bindle (ch. 1)	a bag tied to the end of a long stick that carries a person's belongings	George gently drops his **bindle** to the ground.
morosely (ch. 1)	in a serious, sad, or quiet way	George stares **morosely** at the water hole.
resignedly (ch. 1)	accepting something that cannot be avoided	George reminds Lennie **resignedly** about what happened in Weed.
brusquely (ch. 1)	in a blunt or rough manner	George **brusquely** asks Lennie for the dead mouse.
imperiously (ch. 1)	in a superior or domineering way	George stretches out his hand **imperiously** to Lennie.
craftily (ch. 1)	in a clever or sneaky way	Lennie **craftily** asks George to tell him about the rabbits.

Name ....

Date ....

Understanding Vocabulary Words

Directions: The following words appear in this section of the book. Use context clues and reference materials to determine an accurate definition for each word.

Word	Definition
foothill (ch. 1)	
junctures (ch. 1)	
recumbent (ch. 1)	
tramps (ch. 1)	
bindle (ch. 1)	
morosely (ch. 1)	
resignedly (ch. 1)	
brusquely (ch. 1)	
imperiously (ch. 1)	
craftily (ch. 1)	

Name _____

Date _____

During-Reading Vocabulary Activity

Directions: As you read these chapters, record at least eight important words on the lines below. Try to find interesting, difficult, intriguing, special, or funny words. Your words can be long or short. They can be hard or easy to spell. After each word, use context clues in the text and reference materials to define the word.

- _____
- _____
  _____
- _____
- _____
- _____
- _____
- _____
- _____
- _____
- _____

Directions: Respond to these questions about the words in this section.

1. Why do George and Lennie each carry a **bindle**?

_____

_____

2. Why does George ask **brusquely** for the mouse?

_____

_____

Analyzing the Literature

Provided below are discussion questions you can use in small groups, with the whole class, or for written assignments. Each question is given at two levels so you can choose the right question for each group of students. Activity sheets with these questions are provided (pages 18–19) if you want students to write their responses. For each question, a few key discussion points are provided for your reference.

Story Element	■ Level 1	▲ Level 2	Key Discussion Points
Character	What do George and Lennie physically look like?	How do George's and Lennie's physical descriptions mirror their characters?	George is described as being small and dark with sharp, strong features. Lennie is very large with a shapeless face, sloping shoulders, and pale eyes. This echoes their characters because George is intelligent and controlled while Lennie is slow and awkward.
Setting	Why are George and Lennie camping at night?	Why do you think the author has Lennie and George camp out instead of going to the ranch that night?	The bus driver lets them off far away from the ranch, so they have to walk four miles to the ranch. George wants to relax for the night before going in the morning. Answers may include that the camp scene allows readers to learn about the characters' dreams of owning land. Starting at the ranch would make introducing that specific information more difficult.
Character	What does George say his life would be like without Lennie?	How does Lennie cause trouble for George?	George says that without Lennie, he could keep a job and do whatever he wants—play cards, buy whiskey, or stay at a hotel. Lennie causes them both to lose their jobs. George gives the example that in Weed, Lennie touched a girl's dress and wouldn't let go when she got scared. They ended up hiding from a group of men looking for them.
Plot	Why is the dialogue written in non-standard English?	How does the author's style of writing the dialogue help tell the story?	The dialogue is written to show how George and Lennie actually talk. It helps make the story feel more realistic and shows the readers their characters. Saying things like, "You never oughtta drink water when it ain't running" lets readers know the two men are probably not rich nor highly educated.

Name _____

Date _____

Analyzing the Literature

Directions: Think about the section you just read. Read each question and state your response with textual evidence.

1. What do George and Lennie physically look like?

_____

_____

_____

_____

2. Why are George and Lennie camping at night?

_____

_____

_____

_____

3. What does George say his life would be like without Lennie?

_____

_____

_____

_____

4. Why is the dialogue written in non-standard English?

_____

_____

_____

_____

Name _____

Date _____

▲ Analyzing the Literature

Directions: Think about the section you just read. Read each question and state your response with textual evidence.

1. How do George's and Lennie's physical descriptions mirror their characters?

_____

_____

_____

_____

2. Why do you think the author has Lennie and George camp out instead of going to the ranch that night?

_____

_____

_____

_____

3. How does Lennie cause trouble for George?

_____

_____

_____

_____

4. How does the author's style of writing the dialogue help tell the story?

_____

_____

_____

_____

Name _____

Date _____

Reader Response

Directions: Choose one of the following prompts about this section to answer. Be sure you include a topic sentence in your response, use textual evidence to support your opinion, and provide a strong conclusion that summarizes your opinion.

Writing Prompts

- **Argument Piece**—Would you rather be friends with someone like George or someone like Lennie? Include examples to explain your choice.
- **Informative/Explanatory Piece**—Why do you think George needs a plan about what to do if Lennie gets into trouble? Use the text in your explanation.

_____

_____

_____

_____

_____

_____

_____

_____

_____

_____

_____

_____

_____

_____

_____

Name _____

Date _____

Close Reading the Literature

Directions: Closely reread the section in chapter 1 when George tells Lennie about their future plans. Begin with, "George stared morosely at the fire." Read until he says, "I ain't got time for no more." Read each question and then revisit the text to find evidence that supports your answer.

1. According to the text, how are George and Lennie different from the other workers?

_____

_____

_____

2. Explain why Lennie says, "I could go off in the hills there. Someplace I'd find a cave." Justify your answer using the text to provide evidence.

_____

_____

_____

3. What role does the setting play in this section? Support your answer with textual examples.

_____

_____

_____

4. What does the author want readers to infer about George and Lennie's relationship?

_____

_____

_____

Name _____

Date _____

Making Connections—The Dust Bowl

Directions: Though California was not directly affected by the Dust Bowl, the state was impacted during the Great Depression. Research the Dust Bowl using books or the Internet, and answer the questions below.

1. What caused the Dust Bowl to occur?

_____

_____

2. What were Black Blizzards?

_____

_____

_____

3. What areas were hit the hardest?

_____

_____

4. How did the Dust Bowl affect California?

_____

_____

_____

5. What is one other piece of information you found interesting in your research?

_____

_____

_____

Name _____

Date _____

Creating with the Story Elements

Directions: Thinking about the story elements of character, setting, and plot in a novel is very important to understanding what is happening and why. Complete **one** of the following activities based on what you've read so far. Be creative and have fun!

Characters

Create work cards for George and Lennie. Include their names, skills, and any other information you feel would be important for their potential employers to know.

Setting

Create a map of the place where George and Lennie camp the first night. Include the bus stop, campsite, and ranch. Use the author's description for distance scale.

Plot

Write a letter from George to the woman in the red dress from Weed. Explain and apologize for what happened.

Vocabulary Overview

Ten key words from this section are provided below with definitions and sentences about how the words are used in the book. Choose one of the vocabulary activity sheets (pages 25 or 26) for students to complete as they read this section. Monitor students as they work to ensure the definitions they have found are accurate and relate to the text. Finally, discuss these important vocabulary words with students. If you think these words or other words in the section warrant more time devoted to them, there are suggestions in the introduction for other vocabulary activities (page 5).

Word	Definition	Sentence about Text
scourges (ch. 2)	something that causes trouble and suffering	The yellow can says it will kill lice, roaches, and other **scourges**.
liniment (ch. 2)	a lotion rubbed on the body to relieve pain	George unpacks his **liniment** and puts it on the shelf.
mollified (ch. 2)	reduced the anger or anxiety of someone	George is **mollified** when Candy says he doesn't listen and won't ask any questions.
pugnacious (ch. 2)	eager to argue and fight	Curley's glance is calculating and **pugnacious**.
ominously (ch. 2)	suggesting that something bad could happen	George **ominously** says that Curley should watch out for Lennie.
derogatory (ch. 2)	showing a disrespectful attitude	Candy is reassured when George makes a **derogatory** comment about Curley.
plaintively (ch. 2)	doing something in a sad way	Lennie **plaintively** says he does not want any trouble with Curley.
disengage (ch. 2)	to release something from what it is attached to	Lennie tries to **disengage** his ear from George's grasp.
complacently (ch. 2)	feeling happy and unconcerned	Lennie smiles **complacently** at George's compliment.
mused (ch. 2)	thought about something	Slim **muses** that not many men travel around together.

Name _____

Date _____

Understanding Vocabulary Words

Directions: The following words appear in this section of the book. Use context clues and reference materials to determine an accurate definition for each word.

Word	Definition
scourges (ch. 2)	
liniment (ch. 2)	
mollified (ch. 2)	
pugnacious (ch. 2)	
ominously (ch. 2)	
derogatory (ch. 2)	
plaintively (ch. 2)	
disengage (ch. 2)	
complacently (ch. 2)	
mused (ch. 2)	

Name _____

Date _____

During-Reading Vocabulary Activity

Directions: As you read these chapters, record at least eight important words on the lines below. Try to find interesting, difficult, intriguing, special, or funny words. Your words can be long or short. They can be hard or easy to spell. After each word, use context clues in the text and reference materials to define the word.

- _____
- _____
- _____
- _____
- _____
- _____
- _____
- _____
- _____
- _____

Directions: Respond to these questions about the words in this section.

1. Why is George **mollified** when Candy says he isn't interested in what George is talking about?

   _____

   _____

2. Why does Lennie have to **disengage** his ear from George?

   _____

   _____

Analyzing the Literature

Provided below are discussion questions you can use in small groups, with the whole class, or for written assignments. Each question is given at two levels so you can choose the right question for each group of students. Activity sheets with these questions are provided (pages 28–29) if you want students to write their responses. For each question, a few key discussion points are provided for your reference.

Story Element	■ Level 1	▲ Level 2	Key Discussion Points
Plot	Why is the boss angry with George and Lennie?	Why does the boss say he is going to keep an eye on George?	The boss is angry because George and Lennie arrive late, and the workers are two men short when they go to the fields that morning. The boss is going to keep an eye on George because he does not let Lennie speak, and the boss is suspicious that George is taking Lennie's money.
Character	What is Curley's reaction to George and Lennie?	According to Candy, why is Curley so aggressive with Lennie?	Curley is very angry and aggressive with George and Lennie. He isn't satisfied with George's answers and wants Lennie to speak for himself. Candy says Curley picks on big guys because he is small. If he wins the fight, he will be considered tough; if he loses, everyone will say the big guy should have picked on someone his own size.
Setting	Why do Lennie and George argue about leaving the farm?	Why does Lennie want to leave the farm?	They argue because Lennie wants to leave, but George thinks they should stay and save money. Lennie feels like a lot of bad things have happened since they arrived—the boss wants to keep an eye on them, Curley challenges Lennie, and he gets in trouble with George for saying Curley's wife is pretty.
Character	Describe Curley's wife.	Why do you think the author makes Curley's wife a "tart"?	Curley's wife is described as being pretty but a bit of a troublemaker. She hangs around the bunkhouse and flirts with the workers. Candy refers to her as a "tart." Student answers will vary but may include: Curley's wife is made to be a tart so she will create a problem among the men in the bunkhouse.

Name _____

Date _____

Analyzing the Literature

Directions: Think about the section you just read. Read each question and state your response with textual evidence.

1. Why is the boss angry with George and Lennie?

_____

_____

_____

_____

2. What is Curley's reaction to George and Lennie?

_____

_____

_____

_____

3. Why do Lennie and George argue about leaving the farm?

_____

_____

_____

_____

4. Describe Curley's wife.

_____

_____

_____

_____

Name _____

Date _____

▲ Analyzing the Literature

Directions: Think about the section you just read. Read each question and state your response with textual evidence.

1. Why does the boss say he is going to keep an eye on George?

_____

_____

_____

_____

2. According to Candy, why is Curley so aggressive with Lennie?

_____

_____

_____

_____

3. Why does Lennie want to leave the farm?

_____

_____

_____

_____

4. Why do you think the author made Curley's wife a "tart"?

_____

_____

_____

_____

Name _____

Date _____

Reader Response

Directions: Choose one of the following prompts about this section to answer. Be sure you include a topic sentence in your response, use textual evidence to support your opinion, and provide a strong conclusion that summarizes your opinion.

Writing Prompts

- **Narrative Piece**—George is concerned that Lennie is going to get into trouble. Offer George some advice on how to help Lennie avoid problems.

- **Informative/Explanatory Piece**—Choose one event from this section that could be foreshadowing something to come in the novel. Describe the event and explain your prediction.

_____

_____

_____

_____

_____

_____

_____

_____

_____

_____

_____

_____

_____

Name

Date

Close Reading the Literature

Directions: Closely reread the section in chapter 2 when Candy tells Lennie and George about Curley's wife. Begin when Candy says, "Seems to me like he's worse lately." Stop when George says, "Say it over to yourself, Lennie, so you won't forget it." Read each question, and then revisit the text to find evidence that supports your answer.

1. Why does Candy feel reassured by George's comment about Curley's wife?

_____

_____

_____

2. In this section, Curley's wife is introduced through Candy's description. What inferences can you make about her marriage to Curley using the text?

_____

_____

_____

3. Use the text to explain why George is so angry about Curley's interaction with Lennie.

_____

_____

_____

4. How do the characters' dialogue and actions create the tone of the section? Use textual examples to support your response.

_____

_____

_____

Name

Date

Making Connections–Help Wanted

Directions: Several different jobs around the farm are mentioned in chapter 2. Using the text or an outside resource, learn about each job listed below. Then, create a "Help Wanted" page for a local newspaper advertising each position. Include job requirements, skills needed, pay, and any other important information.

Help Wanted

Swamper	Stable Buck
Bucker	**Jerkline Skinner**

Name _____

Date _____

Creating with the Story Elements

Directions: Thinking about the story elements of character, setting, and plot in a novel is very important to understanding what is happening and why. Complete **one** of the following activities based on what you've read so far. Be creative and have fun!

Characters

Slim is given a thorough description. Make a list of his characteristics. Include five details about his physical features and five details about his personality.

Setting

Create a diagram of the bunkhouse. Use the description from the text as well as your imagination to help you.

Plot

Lennie is very excited about getting a puppy from Slim. Make a job chart for Lennie to help him remember the responsibilities of caring for his new pet.

Vocabulary Overview

Ten key words from this section are provided below with definitions and sentences about how the words are used in the book. Choose one of the vocabulary activity sheets (pages 35 or 36) for students to complete as they read this section. Monitor students as they work to ensure the definitions they have found are accurate and relate to the text. Finally, discuss these important vocabulary words with students. If you think these words or other words in the section warrant more time devoted to them, there are suggestions in the introduction for other vocabulary activities (page 5).

Word	Definition	Sentence about Text
derision (ch. 3)	the feeling associated with insulting or making fun of someone	The men's voices raise in approval or **derision**.
receptive (ch. 3)	willing to consider a new idea	Slim sits back, quiet and **receptive**, to what George says.
rheumatism (ch. 3)	any disease with inflammation and pain in the joints	Candy's dog is stiff with **rheumatism**.
euchre (ch. 3)	a card game played with 24 or 32 cards	George asks the men if they want to play **euchre**.
subdued (ch. 3)	got control of something, such as a strong emotion	Slim **subdues** one hand with the other as he waits.
ejector (ch. 3)	a device in a gun that ejects the empty shell of a bullet	Candy rolls over when he hears the gun's **ejector** snap.
hoosegow (ch. 3)	slang for a prison	George thinks Curley's wife is trouble and will land someone in the **hoosegow**.
reprehensible (ch. 3)	something very bad and deserving a consequence	Lennie and George jump as though they had been caught doing something **reprehensible**.
reverently (ch. 3)	showing solemn respect	George **reverently** says that they might be able to buy the land.
bemused (ch. 3)	puzzled or confused	They are sitting together, **bemused** by the beauty of their dream.

Name _____

Date _____

Understanding Vocabulary Words

Directions: The following words appear in this section of the book. Use context clues and reference materials to determine an accurate definition for each word.

Word	Definition
derision (ch. 3)	
receptive (ch. 3)	
rheumatism (ch. 3)	
euchre (ch. 3)	
subdued (ch. 3)	
ejector (ch. 3)	
hoosegow (ch. 3)	
reprehensible (ch. 3)	
reverently (ch. 3)	
bemused (ch. 3)	

Name _____

Date _____

During-Reading Vocabulary Activity

Directions: As you read these chapters, record at least eight important words on the lines below. Try to find interesting, difficult, intriguing, special, or funny words. Your words can be long or short. They can be hard or easy to spell. After each word, use context clues in the text and reference materials to define the word.

- _____
- _____
  _____
- _____
  _____
- _____
  _____
- _____
  _____
- _____
  _____
- _____
  _____
- _____
  _____
- _____
  _____
- _____

Directions: Now, organize your words. Rewrite each of the words on a sticky note. Work with a group to create a bar graph of your words. Stack any words that are the same on top of one another. Different words should appear in different columns. Finally, discuss with the group why certain words were chosen more often than other words.

Analyzing the Literature

Provided below are discussion questions you can use in small groups, with the whole class, or for written assignments. Each question is given at two levels so you can choose the right question for each group of students. Activity sheets with these questions are provided (pages 38–39) if you want students to write their responses. For each question, a few key discussion points are provided for your reference.

Story Element	■ Level 1	▲ Level 2	Key Discussion Points
Character	When they were younger, why did George stop playing tricks on Lennie?	What does George's treatment of Lennie when they were young show about his character?	George says when he was young, he told Lennie to jump into the river even though he couldn't swim. Lennie almost drowned. When George pulled him out, Lennie thanked him for saving his life. This shows that although George could be mean and a bully, he does have a conscience and can be compassionate.
Setting	How does Candy involve himself in Lennie and George's dream of owning land?	Why does Candy want to join George and Lennie on the farm of their dreams?	Candy overhears George tell Lennie "about the rabbits." Candy can contribute $350 if they let him come along. Candy wants to join them because he is getting old and fears he will be fired when he cannot work anymore. If he is on the farm with George and Lennie, he will have a place to belong.
Plot	Do you think Candy or Carlson should have shot the dog? Why?	Why does Candy say he should have shot his dog?	Student responses will vary but may include: Carlson should have shot the dog because Candy loved it too much to kill it. Candy should have shot the dog because it was his responsibility. Candy feels he owes the dog more respect than to let a stranger shoot it. He feels a responsibility to the dog and should do what is best for it, even if the decision is hard.
Character	How does Lennie prove that no one should fight him?	Why does Curley attack Lennie?	Lennie proves it is dangerous to fight him when he grabs Curley's hand during their fight. He crushes all of the bones and doesn't let go until George slaps him repeatedly. Curley attacks Lennie because he is embarrassed about accusing Slim of being with his wife and angry because the other men are giving him a hard time. He sees Lennie smiling and takes his frustrations out on him.

Name _____

Date _____

Analyzing the Literature

Directions: Think about the section you just read. Read each question and state your response with textual evidence.

1. When they were younger, why did George stop playing tricks on Lennie?

_____

_____

_____

_____

2. How does Candy involve himself in Lennie and George's dream of owning land?

_____

_____

_____

_____

3. Do you think Candy or Carlson should have shot the dog? Why?

_____

_____

_____

_____

4. How does Lennie prove that no one should fight him?

_____

_____

_____

_____

Name _____

Date _____

▲ Analyzing the Literature

Directions: Think about the section you just read. Read each question and state your response with textual evidence.

1. What does George's treatment of Lennie when they were young show about his character?

_____

_____

_____

_____

2. Why does Candy want to join George and Lennie on the farm of their dreams?

_____

_____

_____

_____

3. Why does Candy say he should have shot his dog?

_____

_____

_____

_____

4. Why does Curley attack Lennie?

_____

_____

_____

_____

Name _____

Date _____

Reader Response

Directions: Choose one of the following prompts about this section to answer. Be sure you include a topic sentence in your response, use textual evidence to support your opinion, and provide a strong conclusion that summarizes your opinion.

Writing Prompts

- **Argument Piece**—How do you feel about the shooting of Candy's dog? Include examples from the text to support your opinion.
- **Narrative Piece**—Now that Curley has fought Lennie and lost, discuss what you think their relationship will be like now and how the other men will react.

_____

_____

_____

_____

_____

_____

_____

_____

_____

_____

_____

_____

_____

_____

_____

_____

Name _____

Date _____

Close Reading the Literature

Directions: Closely reread the section in chapter 3 when Carlson talks Candy into shooting his dog. Begin when Carlson says, "Damn right he is." Stop when he says, "He wouldn't even quiver." Read each question and then revisit the text to find evidence that supports your answer.

1. Use the text to compare and contrast Carlson's and Slim's opinions on shooting Candy's dog.

_____

_____

_____

2. Slim is not a main character, so why does the author choose to include him? Support your answer with textual evidence.

_____

_____

_____

3. How do Candy and his dog mirror George and Lennie?

_____

_____

_____

4. Why does Candy resist Carlson's offer to shoot the dog? Use the text to explain your answer.

_____

_____

_____

Name _____

Date _____

Making Connections–Grow Alfalfa

Directions: Lennie dreams of tending the rabbits with alfalfa grown on the farm. You can grow alfalfa, too!

Materials Needed:
- glass jar with ring lid
- water
- cheesecloth or pantyhose
- paper plate
- alfalfa seeds

Steps:

1. Measure two tablespoons of seeds. Throw away any seeds that are broken, withered, or damaged.

2. Put the seeds in the glass jar and cover them with two inches of water. Put the cheesecloth or pantyhose over the top of the jar and screw on the ring lid. Let the seeds soak overnight.

3. Drain the water by turning over the jar in a sink. Roll the jar around until the seeds are stuck to the sides. Store the jar in a dark place on its side.

4. Rinse the seeds twice a day with room temperature water. If the jar starts to smell, rinse the seeds more often.

5. After 4–6 days, the sprouts should be 1–2 inches and are ready to harvest. Put the sprouts on a paper plate and place it in the sun for about 15 minutes. The sunlight will activate enzymes, and the sprouts will begin to turn green.

6. The sprouts are ready to eat on a salad or sandwich. Store any unused sprouts in the refrigerator for up to one week.

Name

Date

Creating with the Story Elements

Directions: Thinking about the story elements of character, setting, and plot in a novel is very important to understanding what is happening and why. Complete **one** of the following activities based on what you've read so far. Be creative and have fun!

Characters

List three characteristics of Candy. Find a sentence from the chapter to support each characteristic.

Setting

Create a "For Sale" brochure for the farm George has found. Include an illustration of the land and house, as well as information about the property, selling points, and price.

Plot

Though it is not in the book, imagine when Curley tells his wife and father about his injury. Create a comic strip about what that scene might be like.

Vocabulary Overview

Ten key words from this section are provided below with definitions and sentences about how the words are used in the book. Choose one of the vocabulary activity sheets (pages 45 or 46) for students to complete as they read this section. Monitor students as they work to ensure the definitions they have found are accurate and relate to the text. Finally, discuss these important vocabulary words with students. If you think these words or other words in the section warrant more time devoted to them, there are suggestions in the introduction for other vocabulary activities (page 5).

Word	Definition	Sentence about Text
accumulated (ch. 4)	gathered together a growing number of things	Crooks **accumulates** more possessions than he can carry on his back.
aloof (ch. 4)	not friendly, uninterested	Crooks is a proud, **aloof** man.
disarming (ch. 4)	removing feelings of distrust or unfriendliness	Lennie's **disarming** smile makes Crooks invite him in.
overwhelmed (ch. 4)	affected someone very strongly	Candy stops talking because he is **overwhelmed** by the picture in his mind.
contemptuously (ch. 4)	without respect	Curley's wife speaks **contemptuously** to the other men about Curley's injury.
indignation (ch. 4)	anger about something thought to be unfair	Curley's wife is breathless with **indignation** while she talks about her chance to be in pictures.
averted (ch. 4)	turned away	Crooks **averts** his eyes while Curley's wife talks to him.
subsided (ch. 4)	became less violent and intense	Candy **subsides** when Curley's wife says no one will believe them.
appraised (ch. 4)	assessed the value of something	Curley's wife **appraises** Candy coolly when he tells her to leave.
crestfallen (ch. 4)	sad and disappointed	Candy is **crestfallen** when George scolds him for telling Crooks about their plan.

Name

Date

Understanding Vocabulary Words

Directions: The following words appear in this section of the book. Use context clues and reference materials to determine an accurate definition for each word.

Word	Definition
accumulated (ch. 4)	
aloof (ch. 4)	
disarming (ch. 4)	
overwhelmed (ch. 4)	
contemptuously (ch. 4)	
indignation (ch. 4)	
averted (ch. 4)	
subsided (ch. 4)	
appraised (ch. 4)	
crestfallen (ch. 4)	

Name _____

Date _____

During-Reading Vocabulary Activity

Directions: As you read these chapters, record at least eight important words on the lines below. Try to find interesting, difficult, intriguing, special, or funny words. Your words can be long or short. They can be hard or easy to spell. After each word, use context clues in the text and reference materials to define the word.

- _____
- _____
- _____
- _____
- _____
- _____
- _____
- _____
- _____
- _____

Directions: Respond to these questions about the words in this section.

1. Why does Crooks act **aloof**?

_____

_____

2. What is it about Lennie that makes him so **disarming**?

_____

_____

Analyzing the Literature

Provided below are discussion questions you can use in small groups, with the whole class, or for written assignments. Each question is given at two levels so you can choose the right question for each group of students. Activity sheets with these questions are provided (pages 48–49) if you want students to write their responses. For each question, a few key discussion points are provided for your reference.

Story Element	■ Level 1	▲ Level 2	Key Discussion Points
Character	Why doesn't Crooks want Lennie to come into his room?	Why does Crooks eventually invite Lennie into his room?	Crooks doesn't want Lennie in his room because he is not allowed in the bunkhouse. Lennie is friendly and doesn't understand the social conventions that would prevent a white man from entering an African American man's room. Crooks is lonely, so he eventually invites Lennie in to sit and talk.
Plot	Why doesn't Crooks believe that George, Lennie, and Candy will buy land?	What makes Crooks begin to believe that George, Lennie, and Candy will buy land?	Crooks doesn't think they will buy land because he has heard men talk about it before, but no one has ever done it. He is pessimistic and jaded from his life on the ranch. When Candy tells him they have the land picked out and money saved in the bank, Crooks begins to take them seriously.
Character	Compare Crooks to Curley's wife.	Describe the power struggle between Crooks and Curley's wife.	Both Crooks and Curley's wife feel lonely and like outsiders at the ranch. Crooks feels empowered because of Lennie and Candy's visit and tells Curley's wife to leave. She belittles him and threatens that she could have him "strung up on a tree" (lynched) if she accuses him of doing anything wrong.
Character	Why do you think Crooks changes his mind about going with George, Lennie, and Candy?	What effect does Curley's wife have on Crooks's desire to leave the ranch with George, Lennie, and Candy?	Student answers will vary but may include: Through her threat, Curley's wife reminds Crooks of his place in society. He quickly submits to her and knows he got caught up in the idea of friends and leaving the ranch. Instead of waiting for the dream to fall apart, he wants to push it away first.

Name _____

Date _____

Analyzing the Literature

Directions: Think about the section you just read. Read each question and state your response with textual evidence.

1. Why doesn't Crooks want Lennie to come into his room?

_____

_____

_____

_____

2. Why doesn't Crooks believe that George, Lennie, and Candy will buy land?

_____

_____

_____

_____

3. Compare Crooks to Curley's wife.

_____

_____

_____

_____

4. Why do you think Crooks changes his mind about going with George, Lennie, and Candy?

_____

_____

_____

_____

Name _____

Date _____

▲ Analyzing the Literature

Directions: Think about the section you just read. Read each question and state your response with textual evidence.

1. Why does Crooks eventually invite Lennie into his room?

_____

_____

_____

_____

2. What makes Crooks begin to believe that George, Lennie, and Candy will buy land?

_____

_____

_____

_____

3. Describe the power struggle between Crooks and Curley's wife.

_____

_____

_____

_____

4. What effect does Curley's wife have on Crooks's desire to leave the ranch with George, Lennie, and Candy?

_____

_____

_____

Name

Date

Reader Response

Directions: Choose one of the following prompts about this section to answer. Be sure you include a topic sentence in your response, use textual evidence to support your opinion, and provide a strong conclusion that summarizes your opinion.

Writing Prompts

• **Argument Piece**—Use evidence from the text to describe why Crooks says, "S'pose Geroge don't come back no more. What'll you do then?"

• **Informative/Explanatory Piece**—Compare Candy from his introduction in the story to the way he acts with Crooks in chapter 4. How has he changed?

_____

_____

_____

_____

_____

_____

_____

_____

_____

_____

_____

_____

_____

_____

_____

Name _____

Date _____

Close Reading the Literature

Directions: Closely reread the section in chapter 4 when Crooks teases Lennie about George leaving. Begin with, "His voice grew soft and persuasive." Stop when Crooks says, "My brothers'd set on a fence rail an' watch 'em—white chickens they was." Read each question and then revisit the text to find evidence that supports your answer.

1. Why does Crooks tease Lennie with thoughts that George might not come back? Use the text to support your inference.

   _____

   _____

   _____

2. How does Crooks know he has gone too far with his teasing?

   _____

   _____

   _____

3. Use Crooks's dialogue to show how his life is different from the other workers' lives.

   _____

   _____

   _____

4. At the end of this section, Crooks says, "I don't know if I was asleep. If some guy was with me, he could tell me I was asleep . . . But I jus' don't know." What does the author mean by this?

   _____

   _____

Name _____

Date _____

Making Connections—Play Horseshoes

Directions: The men on the ranch enjoy playing horseshoes and comment that Crooks, especially, is a very good player. Read through the information about playing horseshoes. Then, answer the questions below.

Materials

- two stakes in the ground, about 40 feet (12.2 meters) apart
- four horseshoes

Rules

- Play with two individuals or two teams of two people.
- Players take turns throwing the horseshoes toward the stakes in the ground, trying to "ring" the stakes.

Scoring

- Horseshoes must be within one "shoe" (about 6 inches or 0.15 meters) to be considered for points.
- The closest horseshoe is worth one point. A leaner, when the shoe is leaning against the stake, is considered the closest.
- A ringer encircles the stake and is worth three points.
- The game is over when a person or team reaches 40 points.

1. Why do you think the men like playing horseshoes on the ranch?

_____

_____

2. What would you change to make the game interesting for youths today?

_____

_____

_____

Name _____

Date _____

Creating with the Story Elements

Directions: Thinking about the story elements of character, setting, and plot in a novel is very important to understanding what is happening and why. Complete **one** of the following activities based on what you've read so far. Be creative and have fun!

Characters

Curley's wife says she could have been in pictures. Imagine that she leaves for Hollywood and becomes an actress. Draw a movie poster of her first starring role.

Setting

Create a chart or Venn diagram to compare and contrast Crooks's room with the bunkhouse.

Plot

Crooks teases Lennie by saying George might not come back. What if Crooks were right? Write a brief dialogue between Lennie and the other workers discussing George's absence.

Vocabulary Overview

Ten key words from this section are provided below with definitions and sentences about how the words are used in the book. Choose one of the vocabulary activity sheets (pages 55 or 56) for students to complete as they read this section. Monitor students as they work to ensure the definitions they have found are accurate and relate to the text. Finally, discuss these important vocabulary words with students. If you think these words or other words in the section warrant more time devoted to them, there are suggestions in the introduction for other vocabulary activities (page 5).

Word	Definition	Sentence about Text
contorted (ch. 5)	twisted out of its normal shape	Lennie's face is **contorted** in panic.
writhed (ch. 5)	made continuous twisting motions with the body	Curley's wife **writhes** in an attempt to get away from Lennie.
discontent (ch. 5)	not satisfied	The **discontent** is gone from Curley's wife's face, and she is pretty and simple.
disapprovingly (ch. 5)	showing an unfavorable opinion	Candy **disapprovingly** tells Curley's wife she should not sleep in the barn.
gingham (ch. 6)	lightweight cotton cloth checked with white and another color	Aunt Clara wears a **gingham** apron with pockets.
haunches (ch. 6)	the upper parts of an animal's rear legs	The rabbit from Lennie's imagination sits on its **haunches**.
belligerently (ch. 6)	in an aggressive manner	Lennie **belligerently** tells the rabbit that George will not beat him.
monotonous (ch. 6)	dull and repetitive without any variety	George's voice is **monotonous** and has no emphasis.
woodenly (ch. 6)	showing no expression	George **woodenly** tells Lennie he could live so easy without him.
dutifully (ch. 6)	acting in a way that is expected or required	Lennie **dutifully** removes his hat when George tells him to.

Name _____

Date _____

Understanding Vocabulary Words

Directions: The following words appear in this section of the book. Use context clues and reference materials to determine an accurate definition for each word.

Word	Definition
contorted (ch. 5)	
writhed (ch. 5)	
discontent (ch. 5)	
disapprovingly (ch. 5)	
gingham (ch. 6)	
haunches (ch. 6)	
belligerently (ch. 6)	
monotonous (ch. 6)	
woodenly (ch. 6)	
dutifully (ch. 6)	

Name _____

Date _____

During-Reading Vocabulary Activity

Directions: As you read these chapters, choose five important words from the story. Then, use those five words to complete this word flow chart. On each arrow, write a vocabulary word. In the boxes between the words, explain how the words connect. An example for the words *contorted* and *writhed* has been done for you.

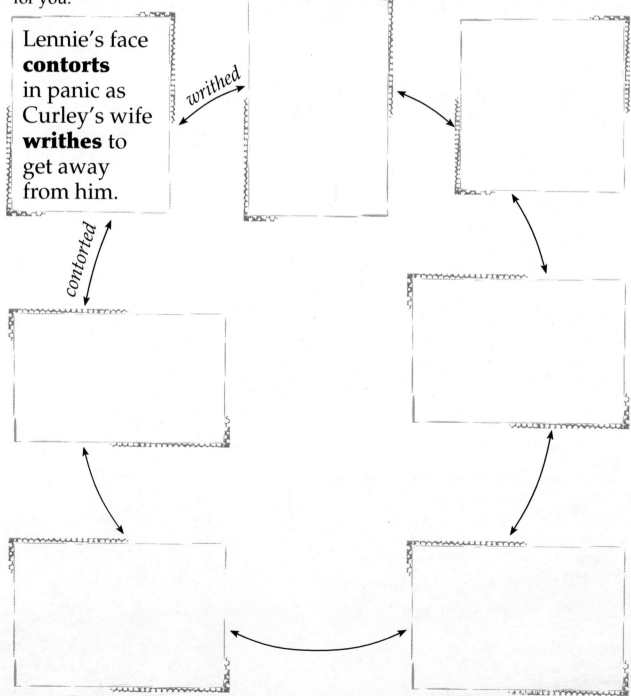

Lennie's face **contorts** in panic as Curley's wife **writhes** to get away from him.

writhed

contorted

Analyzing the Literature

Provided below are discussion questions you can use in small groups, with the whole class, or for written assignments. Each question is given at two levels so you can choose the right question for each group of students. Activity sheets with these questions are provided (pages 58–59) if you want students to write their responses. For each question, a few key discussion points are provided for your reference.

Story Element	■ Level 1	▲ Level 2	Key Discussion Points
Character	How is Curley's wife's death similar to what happened in Weed?	How does knowing what happened in Weed help explain what Lennie did to Curley's wife?	In Weed, Lennie touched a woman's soft dress and didn't let go when she tried to pull away. Curley's wife's death is similar, as Lennie doesn't let go of her hair when she pulls away. The story helps explain that when Lennie is scared or confused, he grabs objects and cannot be reasoned with.
Setting	Why does George know where to find Lennie?	How does the brush serve as foreshadowing in the book?	George is able to find Lennie because the night before arriving at the ranch, he told Lennie to hide in the brush if he got in trouble. Several times in the book, Lennie mentions the brush. This foreshadows that he will be in trouble and will need to go there.
Plot	Why do you think Lennie is having hallucinations with Aunt Clara and the rabbit?	What do you think each of Lennie's hallucinations show about his thoughts?	Possible answers: Lennie is scared and upset, which could bring on hallucinations. His thoughts are coming out in the form of his aunt and the rabbit. The Aunt Clara hallucination shows that he is afraid he makes George's life worse, and the rabbit shows he is afraid George is going to be very angry and hurt him.
Character	How does Slim show friendship to George?	Compare and contrast Slim's reaction to Lennie's death with Curley's and Carlson's reactions.	Slim shows friendship to George by sitting close to him, reassuring him, and offering to get him a drink. By extending kindness to George, Slim shows he understands the situation. Curley and Carlson are pleased Lennie is dead and feel justice has been served. They do not realize the effect the death has on George.

Name _____

Date _____

Analyzing the Literature

Directions: Think about the section you just read. Read each question and state your response with textual evidence.

1. How is Curley's wife's death similar to what happened in Weed?

_____

_____

_____

_____

2. Why does George know where to find Lennie?

_____

_____

_____

_____

3. Why do you think Lennie is having hallucinations with Aunt Clara and the rabbit?

_____

_____

_____

_____

4. How does Slim show friendship to George?

_____

_____

_____

_____

Name _____

Date _____

▲ Analyzing the Literature

Directions: Think about the section you just read. Read each question and state your response with textual evidence.

1. How does knowing what happened in Weed help explain what Lennie did to Curley's wife?

   _____

   _____

   _____

   _____

2. How does the brush serve as foreshadowing in the book?

   _____

   _____

   _____

   _____

3. What do you think each of Lennie's hallucinations show about his thoughts?

   _____

   _____

   _____

   _____

4. Compare and contrast Slim's reaction to Lennie's death with Curley's and Carlson's reactions.

   _____

   _____

   _____

Name _____

Date _____

Reader Response

Directions: Choose one of the following prompts about this section to answer. Be sure you include a topic sentence in your response, use textual evidence to support your opinion, and provide a strong conclusion that summarizes your opinion.

Writing Prompts

- **Narrative**—George faces a tough decision after Lennie kills Curley's wife. If you were George, what would you do?
- **Informative/Explanatory Piece**—Earlier in the book, Candy says he should have been the one to shoot his dog. Compare and contrast this earlier scene to what happens with George and Lennie.

_____

_____

_____

_____

_____

_____

_____

_____

_____

_____

_____

_____

_____

_____

_____

Name _____

Date _____

Close Reading the Literature

Directions: Closely reread in chapter 5 when all of the workers discover Curley's wife is dead. Begin when Candy asks, "What we gonna do now, George?" Stop when George says, "I know." Read each question and then revisit the text to find evidence that supports your answer.

1. According to Candy, why can they not let Lennie get away?

_____

_____

_____

2. How does this section show that George needs Lennie? Use textual evidence in your answer.

_____

_____

_____

3. What emotions does Candy experience during this section? Include details from the text to support your response.

_____

_____

_____

_____

4. According to Slim, why can they not let Lennie go to jail?

_____

_____

_____

Name _____

Date _____

Making Connections—The Hero's Journey

Directions: Create a review of the novel *Of Mice and Men*. First, rate it on a scale of 1–5 stars (5 being the best), and then write a paragraph explaining your thoughts and opinions about the book. Be sure to include what you do or do not like about the book, anything you learned or found interesting, who might enjoy reading it, and your general feelings about the novel.

_____
_____
_____
_____
_____
_____
_____
_____
_____
_____
_____
_____
_____
_____
_____
_____

Name _____

Date _____

Creating with the Story Elements

Directions: Thinking about the story elements of character, setting, and plot in a novel is very important to understanding what is happening and why. Complete **one** of the following activities based on what you've read so far. Be creative and have fun!

Characters

Write a eulogy for Curley's wife from the perspective of Curley, Slim, or Candy.

Setting

Imagine the novel was written recently. List ten things that would be different in the new, modern-day setting.

Plot

Create a police report detailing the incident between Lennie and Curley's wife in the barn. Be sure to include witness statements and medical information.

Name _____

Date _____

Post-Reading Theme Thoughts

Directions: Read each of the statements in the first column. Choose a main character from *Of Mice and Men*. Think about that character's point of view. From that character's perspective, decide if the character would agree or disagree with the statements. Record the character's opinion by marking an *X* in Agree or Disagree for each statement. Explain your choices in the fourth column using text evidence.

Character I Chose: _____

Statement	Agree	Disagree	Explain Your Answer
You can make your dreams come true by working hard.			
It is better to be with others than to be by yourself.			
Sometimes there is no good solution to a problem.			
People with intellectual disabilities should not be responsible for their actions.			

Name _____

Date _____

Culminating Activity: Lights, Camera, Action!

Overview: John Steinbeck adapted *Of Mice and Men* for the stage while it was still on the bestseller list. On November 23, 1937, the play premiered on Broadway. Since then, it has had revival performances on Broadway in 1974, 1987, and 2014. It was also made into movies in 1939 and 1992.

Directions: To prepare for your next activity, use resources to determine a brief description for each production job. Then, answer the question below.

Actor _____

_____

Director _____

_____

Costume Designer _____

_____

Set Decorator/Props _____

_____

1. Describe three scenes from the book that you think would work well in a play or movie.

_____

_____

_____

_____

_____

_____

Name _____

Date _____

Culminating Activity: Lights, Camera, Action! (cont.)

Directions: In a group of 4–6 people, perform a scene from *Of Mice and Men*. You may film your scene and play the recording for your class or perform it live. Group members might need to have more than one job. Use the table on this page to help your group plan its production. Write the scene on a separate sheet of paper. Work cooperatively with your group members, be creative, and have fun!

Actor	Director
Name(s):	Name(s):
Notes:	Notes:
Costume Designer	**Set Decorator/Props**
Name(s):	Name(s):
Notes:	Notes:

Write a brief description of your group's chosen scene:

_____

_____

_____

Name _____

Date _____

Comprehension Assessment

Directions: Circle the letter for the best response to each question.

1. What is the meaning of *tart* as used in the book?

    A. a pastry with filling

    B. a woman who behaves in a provocative way

    C. a person who is mentally ill

    D. a derogatory term for an African American

2. Which detail from the book best supports your answer to question 1?

    E. "I seen her give Slim the eye . . . An' I seen her give Carlson the eye."

    F. "You guys better come on while they's still something to eat."

    G. "I could get you strung up on a tree so easy it ain't even funny."

    H. "It jus' seems kinda funny a cuckoo like him and a smart little guy like you travelin' together."

3. What is the main idea of the text below?

    "Guys like us, that work on ranches, are the loneliest guys in the world. They got no family. They don't belong no place . . . With us it ain't like that. We got a future. We got somebody to talk to that gives a damn about us."

    _____

    _____

    _____

    _____

4. Choose **two** details to support your answer to number 3.

    E. "Maybe he ain't bright, but I never seen such a worker."

    F. "I never seen one guy take so much trouble for another guy."

    G. "It ain't so funny, him an' me goin' aroun' together."

    H. "I'm scared I'm gonna tangle with that bastard myself."

Comprehension Assessment (cont.)

5. Which statement best expresses a theme of the book?

   A. Friendship is important.

   B. People can change their lives if they work hard.

   C. Smart people are not nice.

   D. Enemies are easily made.

6. What detail from the book provides the best evidence for your answer to number 5?

   E. "But we gonna do it now, and don't make no mistake about that."

   F. "Guy don't need no sense to be a nice fella."

   G. "A guy needs somebody—to be near him."

   H. "I hate that kinda bastard . . . I seen plenty of 'em."

7. What is the purpose of these sentences from the book:

   "If you don't want me I can go off in the hills an' find a cave. I can go away any time."

   "No—look! I was jus' foolin', Lennie. 'Cause I want you to stay with me."

   _____

   _____

   _____

   _____

8. Which other quotation from the story serves a similar purpose?

   A. "He can't think of nothing to do himself, but he sure can take orders."

   B. "It ain't your fault . . . You don't need to be scairt no more."

   C. "I don't blame the guy you travel with for keepin' you outta sight."

   D. "But you get used to goin' around with a guy an' you can't get rid of him."

Response to Literature: Equality for All

Overview: Published in 1937, *Of Mice and Men* depicts a realistic portrayal of life for migrant workers during the Great Depression. In addition, the novel uses three distinct characters to show how certain groups of people were treated during this time. Lennie, a person with a disability; Curley's wife, a woman; and Crooks, an African American, are all treated differently from the other workers for reasons beyond their control.

One way people work for change and equality is through new laws. Two of these laws are listed below.

- **Americans with Disabilities Act**—Passed in 1990, this act outlaws discrimination based on a mental or physical disability. It also requires employers to provide reasonable accommodations to people with disabilities.

- **Civil Rights Act**—This bill was signed into law in 1964. It makes discrimination based on race, color, religion, sex, or national origin illegal.

Directions: Choose one of the characters and the law that best represents his or her group. Compare and contrast how the character is treated in the book to how that person might be treated today. How has the law affected his/her role in society? Is the group you chose treated equally today? Why or why not? Write a researched essay showing your understanding of the law and how it has changed how people are treated. Use facts and details from the law, and cite the novel to support your thinking. In conclusion, explain your opinion about the question, "Is true equality possible?"

Your essay response to literature should follow these guidelines:

- Be at least 1,000 words in length.
- Cite information about the law.
- Compare/contrast treatment of the character in the novel and similar people today.
- Cite at least three references from the novel.
- Provide a conclusion that summarizes your thoughts and findings.

Final essays are due on _____.

Name _____

Date _____

Response to Literature Rubric

Directions: Use this rubric to evaluate student responses.

	Exceptional Writing	Quality Writing	Developing Writing
Focus and Organization	☐ States a clear opinion and elaborates well. Engages the reader from the opening hook through the middle to the conclusion. Demonstrates clear understanding of the intended audience and purpose of the piece.	☐ Provides a clear and consistent opinion. Maintains a clear perspective and supports it through elaborating details. Makes the opinion clear in the opening hook and summarizes well in the conclusion.	☐ Provides an inconsistent point of view. Does not support the topic adequately or misses pertinent information. Provides lack of clarity in the beginning, middle, and conclusion.
Text Evidence	☐ Provides comprehensive and accurate support. Includes relevant and worthwhile text references.	☐ Provides limited support. Provides few supporting text references.	☐ Provides very limited support for the text. Provides no supporting text references.
Written Expression	☐ Uses descriptive and precise language with clarity and intention. Maintains a consistent voice and uses an appropriate tone that supports meaning. Uses multiple sentence types and transitions well between ideas.	☐ Uses a broad vocabulary. Maintains a consistent voice and supports a tone and feelings through language. Varies sentence length and word choices.	☐ Uses a limited and unvaried vocabulary. Provides an inconsistent or weak voice and tone. Provides little to no variation in sentence type and length.
Language Conventions	☐ Capitalizes, punctuates, and spells accurately. Demonstrates complete thoughts within sentences, with accurate subject-verb agreement. Uses paragraphs appropriately and with clear purpose.	☐ Capitalizes, punctuates, and spells accurately. Demonstrates complete thoughts within sentences and appropriate grammar. Paragraphs are properly divided and supported.	☐ Incorrectly capitalizes, punctuates, and spells. Uses fragmented or run-on sentences. Utilizes poor grammar overall. Paragraphs are poorly divided and developed.

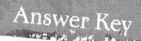
Answer Key

The responses provided here are just examples of what the students may answer. Many accurate responses are possible for the questions throughout this unit.

During-Reading Vocabulary Activity—Section 1:
Chapter 1 (page 16)

1. George and Lennie carry **bindles** because they do not have a permanent home, and the bindles hold their belongings.

2. George asks **brusquely** for the dead mouse because he already threw it away once and is annoyed that Lennie went and got it again.

Close Reading the Literature—Section 1:
Chapter 1 (page 21)

1. George says the other guys work alone and when they get their money at the end of the month, they spend it on frivolous things with no long-term goals. George and Lennie have each other, and they have a dream of buying a small farm and growing crops.

2. Lennie says this to George as a kind of game. He won't really leave George, but is trying to use reverse psychology to make George say he wants Lennie to stay. The text says Lennie "avoided the bait" after George offers him a puppy and that he "sensed his advantage" during their disagreement.

3. The setting plays an important role in illustrating the lifestyle of George and Lennie. They are outdoors in the farm country of 1930s California. The setting gives them the opportunity to camp and talk. Their dream of owning land is also based on the setting.

4. The author wants readers to infer that the two men need each other. George is the leader and acts as if having Lennie around is an inconvenience, but given the choice, he genuinely wants Lennie to stay. Lennie idolizes George and wants to please him but also knows how to annoy him.

Making Connections—Section 1:
Chapter 1 (page 22)

1. The Dust Bowl was caused by years of drought in the 1930s. The soil was dry and dusty, and the crops had weak, shallow roots. A massive windstorm swept through the Midwest and destroyed crops and homes.

2. Black Blizzards were the windstorms that swirled the dirt and debris around the land.

3. The hardest hit areas were Kansas, western Oklahoma, and Texas. Parts of Colorado and New Mexico were also hit.

4. With their homes destroyed and crops ruined, families fled to other parts of the country. Many of them headed to California, causing the issue of too many people and not enough jobs.

5. Student responses will vary.

During-Reading Vocabulary Activity—Section 2:
Chapter 2 (page 26)

1. George is **mollified** because he is worried Candy was eavesdropping on his conversation. When Candy says he doesn't listen or ask questions, George feels more comfortable.

2. Lennie has to **disengage** his ear because George grabs it when Lennie says how pretty Curley's wife is.

Close Reading the Literature—Section 2:
Chapter 2 (page 31)

1. Candy has been gossiping and sharing information about Curley's wife with George. If George were to tell someone, Candy could get in trouble. Now that George has also said something derogatory about Curley's wife, Candy feels they are even. If necessary, he could share what George said and get him in trouble, too.

2. Curley and his wife do not seem to have a strong start to their new marriage. According to Candy, Curley's wife hangs around the bunkhouse and flirts with the workers. Candy calls her a tart. George describes Curley as having "ants in his pants," suggesting he is jealous and insecure in his relationship.

3. George is angry because he does not like Curley. He feels that Curley bullies people larger than him because he cannot lose. He is also afraid that Curley will try to fight Lennie, and they will lose their jobs.

4. The tone of this section is very stressful. George tries to be calm and pretends a "lack of interest" when speaking with Candy about Curley and his wife. When Candy leaves, however, George is yelling about Curley and telling Lennie to stay away from Curley, but to hit him if Curley starts a fight. Lennie is confused by George's instructions and is worried that he is in trouble again.

Making Connections—Section 2:
Chapter 2 (page 32)

• The **swamper** is a person who performs odd jobs and does unskilled maintenance in a workplace.

• The **stable buck** cares for the horses and is the lowest position in the stable.

• The **bucker** lifts, carries, or loads crops.

• The **jerkline skinner** drives a team of mules and handles the reigns.

Close Reading the Literature—Section 3:
Chapter 3 (page 41)

1. Carlson and Slim both think the dog should be shot. Carlson thinks this because he doesn't like the smell of the dog, but he says it is because the dog is too old. Slim feels compassionate and tells Candy that the dog is old and unhealthy. Slim says he wishes someone would shoot him if he ever gets as old and sick as the dog, implying it would be a kindness to end his life.

2. The author includes Slim because he is the leader and moral compass of the men in the bunkhouse. He is logical and described as being calm. They respect his opinion; in fact, the text says, "Slim's opinions were law."

3. Candy and George are both devoted to their companion, even if others do not understand why. Each partnership has existed for a long time. The dog and Lennie can make things more difficult for Candy and George, and although Candy and George will admit the faults in their companions, they still want to be with them.

4. Candy loves his dog, though he doesn't admit it. He repeatedly states that he's had the dog since he was a pup. He knows his dog is old and sick, but the idea of getting rid of him is hard to accept.

During-Reading Vocabulary Activity—Section 4:
Chapter 4 (page 46)

1. Crooks acts **aloof** because, as an African American, the other men do not treat him as an equal. His aloofness is a way to protect himself from the others.

2. Lennie is **disarming** because Crooks can tell he is sincerely nice. He is not smart, so Crooks does not feel defensive or intimidated by him.

Close Reading the Literature—Section 4:
Chapter 4 (page 51)

1. Crooks feels left out because he is African American and can't live in the bunkhouse with the others. He is jealous of George and Lennie's companionship and thinks he will make himself feel better by scaring Lennie. The text shows this when Crooks talks about a man needing to be around other men and when he reminisces about his childhood with his two brothers.

2. Crooks knows he has gone too far when Lennie becomes angry and moves toward Crooks, demanding to know who hurt George. He quickly reassures Lennie that George is not hurt and will come back.

3. Crooks lives by himself in his room. He can play horseshoes with the others outside, but when it gets dark, he can't go into their bunkhouse. He must go to his room and read books, which is a lonely and solitary existence.

4. The quotation means that Crooks is so lonely, he sometimes isn't sure what is real. Needing a friend isn't just for the big moments in life, but the small ones, too. Crooks doesn't have anyone to tell him what is right or if someone else is seeing what he sees. He doesn't even know when he is really sleeping, because there is no one to tell him.

Making Connections—Section 4:
Chapter 4 (page 52)

1. The men like to play horseshoes because the equipment is easy for them to get, and it is a way for them to relax after working all day.

2. Answers will vary.

Close Reading the Literature—Section 5:
Chapters 5–6 (page 61)

1. The men can't let Lennie get away because Candy knows Curley will hunt him down and will want to lynch Lennie. Curley is a fighter and wants to get even with Lennie for hurting his hand.

2. George needs Lennie because their relationship makes him different from the other workers. George tells Candy that now he will be like all the other working men—he will spend his money at the end of each month on girls and playing pool.

3. Candy feels disappointment when George says no to buying the farm. The text says, "Before George answered, Candy dropped his head and looked down at the hay." This shows he knows the effect Lennie's actions will have on their plans. Later in the section, Candy feels angry with Curley's wife, accusing her of ruining everything. He feels empty and sad as he repeats George's happy story about how things were going to be at their new place.

4. Slim understands Lennie's intellectual disability and realizes Lennie won't just go to jail like an ordinary person. He says Lennie will be strapped down and locked in a cage, and that isn't the way to live.

Comprehension Assessment (pages 67–68)

1. B. a woman who behaves in a provocative way

2. E. "I seen her give Slim the eye . . . An' I seen her give Carlson the eye."

3. The main idea is that George and Lennie are different from the others because they are a family.

4. F. "I never seen one guy take so much trouble for another guy." G. "It ain't so funny, him an' me goin' aroun' together."

5. A. Friendship is important.

6. G. "A guy needs somebody—to be near him."

7. These sentences show that George needs Lennie as much as Lennie needs George. It's easy to see that Lennie needs George to help him through life, but George also needs the companionship and shared dreams he gets from his relationship with Lennie.

8. D. "But you get used to goin' around with a guy an' you can't get rid of him."